Praying Thru
The Tabernacle

A Biblical Model for Effective Prayer

Jon Courson

Praying Thru the Tabernacle
A Biblical Model for Effective Prayer

Published by Searchlight

Illustrations by B.A.S. Hyytinen

First printing, 2006
Second Printing, 2007
Third Printing, 2012

All Scripture quotations in this book are taken from the King James Version of the Bible.

ISBN-13: 978-0-9789472-0-0
ISBN-10: 0-9789472-0-7

Printed in the United States of America

Contents

❧   ❧   ❧   ❧   ❧

Preface

❧   ❧   ❧   ❧   ❧

The Tabernacle was the portable place of worship the Jews carried with them through the desert after they were released from bondage in Egypt. After the Jews entered the Promised Land, it continued to serve as a place of worship until the Temple was built in the days of Solomon.

As Moses was on Mount Sinai, God spent forty days giving him the Law and the blueprints for the Tabernacle. And while it won't take you forty days or even forty minutes to read this book, my prayer is that the pattern of prayer as seen in the Tabernacle will travel with you on your own pilgrimage this side of the glorious Promised Land that awaits us in heaven.

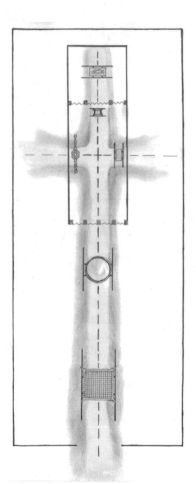

A Walk Thru
The Tabernacle

ঌ   ঌ   ঌ   ঌ   ঌ

L ord, teach us to pray," the disciples said. It was the only recorded lesson they ever requested of Jesus. As far as we know, they never said, "Lord, teach us to preach, teach us to multiply bread, or teach us to heal." Why? I am convinced it is because they realized that everything Jesus did was the direct result of His prayer life.

They would see Him slip away a great while before daybreak to pray. They knew He was on the mountain praying the night they were toiling at the oars in the storm. Even Judas Iscariot knew that when things were coming down and looking dark, he could find Jesus in the Garden of Gethsemane, in the place He frequently went to pray.

Like the disciples, we understand the importance of prayer. Yet most of us are also very keenly aware of the impotence of prayer in our own lives. We know we ought to be people who pray. We want to be people who pray. But, all too often, we are like the disciples who, when Jesus said, "Watch and pray," fell asleep.

"Lord," the disciples said, "teach us to pray."

And such is the cry of our own hearts. We understand the power of prayer — and yet we struggle with prayer. I think I know why this is. The enemy would rather have us do just about anything than pray. He would rather we preach than pray. He would rather we read a good Christian book than pray. He would rather we talk to someone about spiritual things than pray because he knows prayer is where the power is. So he distracts us with seemingly good things to keep us away from the best.

To counter this, the Lord showed me something that has been incredibly helpful for me. Years ago, when I was teaching through the Old Testament, He spoke to my heart in a very real way concerning the use of the Tabernacle as a pattern for prayer.

The Tabernacle — constructed according to God's specifications and described in Exodus 25 through 40 — was essentially a portable sanctuary. It was a tent made of a wooden framework and covered with animal skins. Although it included a courtyard and seven pieces of furniture, it was simple enough to be repeatedly assembled and disassembled as the Israelites journeyed through the wilderness. Yet it was beautiful beyond description with fine gold and exquisite embroidery. The Tabernacle was the place of meeting — where God's people could offer sacrifice and prayer, where they could commune with God. For us as New Testament believers, I believe it provides, in a sense, a place where we can meet with God as well.

Every parent knows that kids love books that have a picture on every page. Our heavenly Father knows the same thing about us, His children. Consequently, the Bible — particularly the Old Testament – is one big picture book. All of the stories and sacrifices, feasts and festivals, battles and biographies are pictures that illustrate spiritual principles because our Father knows we have trouble seeing things abstractly.

Now the Tabernacle is a beautiful example of this precept. As we shall see, the Tabernacle proves to be a truly wonderful picture of the spiritual principles and practices that relate to prayer. It can indeed provide a practical paradigm, a concise but complete pattern, a step-by-step program for the believer to pray most effectively.

Therefore, let me invite you to join with me on a step-by-step walk through the Tabernacle, stopping at each of its eight main components that will provide for us a practical eight step pattern for prayer.

Oh, and remember the words of our Lord who said, "Happy are ye if ye do these things" (John 13:17). So rather than just reading straight through this brief book, why not experience the incredible joy and undeniable blessing that will come in doing the aspect of prayer talked about in each chapter before you go on to the next.

As you do, you will be most blessed. You watch, you wait, you'll see!

Step 1
The Gate

ح‍ح   ح‍ح   ح‍ح   ح‍ح   ح‍ح

The place of thanksgiving

Enter into His gates with thanksgiving . . .
Psalm 100:4

The Tabernacle was a tent 45 feet by 15 feet and surrounded by an enclosure 150 feet by 75 feet. When the Lord gave these dimensions to Moses on Mt. Sinai, I wonder if Moses didn't say, or at least think, "Lord, You're making a mistake. We have three million people in camp on their way to the Promised Land. This is the place we're to meet with You and worship You. Yet You're making it only 150 feet by 75 feet? Isn't that rather small?"

And if indeed Moses voiced those concerns, I wonder if the Lord didn't whisper in his heart, "It will be big enough — for at any given time, not many people will choose to expend the energy, take the time, or make the effort to come and seek Me."

Now the Courtyard was fenced in by a linen curtain. According to Ezekiel 44, linen was also the material of the priests' garments. Why? Because the Lord said the priests were to wear nothing of wool, nothing that caused them to sweat. I like that! There's not to be sweat in ministry or service. Anything we do in serving the Lord should be enjoyable and cool. If it's burdensome, obligatory, or heavy; if it causes you to perspire and worry, it's not what you're called to do.

"My burden is easy and My load is light," Jesus said. This not only relates to ministry, but also to coming into the presence of God.

God was not saying, "Figure out how to get in. Work hard. Struggle. And maybe I'll give you an audience." No. In making a fence of linen, it was as though God was saying, "I am making it as easy as possible for you to come into My presence."

How were God's people to enter into the Courtyard of the Tabernacle? The Bible says they were to enter His Gates with thanksgiving (Psalm 100). Therefore, I like to begin my prayer time by thanking the Lord as well.

Thanksgiving is so important. When people ask me how to find God's will for their lives, I often answer, "In everything give thanks, for this is the will of God in Christ Jesus concerning you" (1 Thessalonians 5:18). Thanksgiving is always a good place to begin.

Why does God desire for us to give thanks in everything? Why does the psalmist declare that it is good to give thanks to the Lord? Because oftentimes we can find ourselves feeling heavy or weighed down, and the key to the suppression of depression is not to pop a pill, but to thank the Lord. Begin to thank the Lord for specific things. Thank Him that you're alive, that your molecular structure is not that of a slug or a dirt clod, that you've been given eternal life — and watch the clouds of depression begin to part.

Paul and Silas certainly found this to be true. With beaten, bloody backs, they were tossed into a Roman prison as punishment for preaching the gospel. Yet, as they sang songs to the Lord, as they entered His Gates with thanksgiving, it wasn't long before they walked out of the prison gates, rejoicing (Acts 16).

The same will be true for you. The dungeon doors of depression will swing open in the midnight hour if you begin to thank God and express your gratitude to Him. You see, a grateful man will always be a great, full man. You know this to be true. The greatest, fullest people you've known are people who are grateful.

First Thessalonians 5:18 tells us we are to give thanks in everything. In addition to this, Ephesians 5:20 says we are to give thanks for everything. I can either choose to be depressed or to give thanks in everything and for everything. If I choose the latter, I suddenly find myself much freer to pray than when I was grumpy and glum.

A good way to begin your prayer time, dear brother or sister, is to give thanks in everything and to give thanks for everything. Then watch and see how that will lubricate the wheels of prayer.

The Courtyard

❧ ❧ ❧ ❧ ❧

The place of praise

... and into His courts with praise . . .
Psalm 100:4

After entering the Gate of the Tabernacle with thanksgiving, I enter the Courtyard with praise. That is, after spending time thanking the Lord for what He has done, I praise Him for who He is. Again, as articulately and specifically as possible, I praise my Father for His beauty, purity and creativity, for His mercy, grace, and love, for His faithfulness, His holiness, His kindness.

Why does God want us to praise Him? Is it because He's unsure of Himself? Is it because He's insecure? Of course not. We praise God not to give Him strokes of affirmation but to foster within our own hearts a spirit of expectation. Remembering the nature of my Father causes me to come to Him with great confidence.

When I begin to pour out my burdens and my questions to the Lord, if I have already exalted Him for being omnipotent and compassionate, I need not wonder if He'll be strong or loving enough to answer my prayer. Praising God for who He is gives me confidence that the burdens that are so heavy to me are no problem for Him.

The people of Judah were surrounded by the Ammonites, the Edomites, and the Moabites. The situation looked grim indeed. But Jahaziel, a prophet of God, said to Jehoshaphat, king of Judah, "Believe the word of the Lord. He will see you through." So Jehoshaphat called for the choir, and the choir went out into the face of the battle. "Praise ye the Lord," they sang. "His mercy endures forever." This so confused the Ammonites, Edomites, and Moabites that they unsheathed their swords and turned their weapons upon each other. The enemy was confused and defeated not when the troops came out swinging, but when the choir came out singing (2 Chronicles 20).

We've experienced the same phenomenon, haven't we? The depression and oppression of demonic entities that surround us actually flee when we begin to praise God. Satan seems to run at the sound of praise.

Why?

I suggest it might be that praise reminds him of who he once was: Lucifer, the worship leader of heaven before he rebelled and was cast out. Therefore, I wonder if when Satan and his hellish henchmen hear praise it doesn't sound to them like fingernails on a chalkboard or the drone of a dentist's drill does to us. I wonder if the sound of praise irritates Satan because it stirs within him memories of the heavenly life that was his before the dust of earth became his home.

There is a difference between thanksgiving and praise. Thanksgiving thanks God for what He does for us. Praise acknowledges who He is to us. God does not need praise. It is we who need to praise so that we remember the nature of the One to whom we bring our requests.

I am reminded of the strength and love of the One to whom I pray when I enter His Courts with praise.

Step 3
The Brass Altar

ক্ক ক্ক ক্ক ক্ক ক্ক

The place of confession

For the life of the flesh is in the blood:
and I have given it to you upon the altar
to make an atonement for your souls . . .
Leviticus 17:11

In the Courtyard of the Tabernacle stood a Brass Altar. This was where the Israelites would bring their sin and trespass offerings. As they placed their hand upon the bullock, goat, or lamb they brought as a sacrifice, they would confess their sin — not generically, but specifically. Then they would watch as the throat of the animal was slit and the blood drained. The animal laid upon the Brass Altar would be an indelible picture of the result of their sin.

In this paradigm for prayer, the Brass Altar is the place where confession is made.

The Greek word for "confess" is *homologeo*. *Homo* means "the same." *Logeo* means "to speak." Thus, confession literally means "to speak the same."

Confession does not mean that we promise never to sin again — because in us dwells no good thing (Romans 7:18). Therefore, to promise not to sin again is a promise that is impossible for us to keep. Confession is simply agreeing with God, saying the same thing He says.

What does God say? He says sin is not a disease, not a vulnerability, not a weakness. It's sin. It's not borrowing — it's stealing. It's not stretching the truth — it's lying. It's not an affair — it's adultery.

Confession says, "Father, I agree with You that this thought or action is sin. It causes erosion within me. It's destructive to my family. It's harmful for the kingdom. It's not right."

Again, be specific. Don't say, "Forgive me for all my sins today," or, "Forgive me for not loving the way I should." Say, "Forgive me for lying to her," or, "Forgive me for hating him." That's honest confession. True confession is very specific. When we learn to confess our sins specifically, we are freed emotionally.

There is a second aspect of confession, one that is often overlooked — and that is confession that we are forgiven.

To the woman caught in the act of adultery, Jesus said, "Woman, where are your accusers? Hath no man condemned thee?"

"No man," she said.

"Neither do I condemn thee," said the Lord (John 8:11).

So too, because of Calvary, I know that the Lord doesn't condemn me (Romans 8:1).

It's not that our confession brings for-giveness, for on the cross Jesus cried, "It is fin-ished." He secured our salvation. He paid for our sin — past, present, and future — when He shed His blood.

All manner of sin is already forgiven all men, Jesus said, except the blasphemy of the Spirit — the rejection of the Son (Matthew 12:31).

What, then, is the purpose of confession? Confession in the life of the believer serves two important purposes. First, it provides liberation from sin.

"Roll away the stone," Jesus said at the tomb of Lazarus.

"Lord," Martha protested "by this time he

stinketh" (John 11:39).

Confession in our lives "rolls away the stone" that we so deliberately place over the tomb of our sin in an attempt to cover it up and mask its stench. You see, Lazarus could not come forth until the stone was removed.

So too, we will be held prisoner by whatever sin we choose to hide rather than confess.

All too often, we, like Martha, protest that our sin is too gross to expose, too bad to uncover. "It stinks," we protest. But there can be no victory, no real resurrection without honest, open, transparent confession.

Confession provides liberation. It rolls away the stone and transforms that which once reeked of death into a sweet savor of life (2 Corinthians 2:15, 16).

In addition to providing liberation from our sin, confession fosters an appreciation for our Savior. In Luke 7, Jesus told Simon the Pharisee that "the one who is forgiven much loves much." When I fail to confess my sin specifically and thoughtfully, I don't realize just how much I am forgiven. And I won't really realize the depth of His incredible, unconditional, sacrificial love for me personally. But if I am truly confessing, I will indeed be blown away by His mercy and grace and "love much."

Now please note, to "love much," we don't need to sin more. We already sin plenty! What we need to do is confess with more specificity and honesty, to rediscover daily just how much we're being forgiven. This will cause us to "love much" our Merciful Master!

The Brass Laver

ò   ò   ò   ò   ò

The place of meditation

*Now ye are clean through the Word
which I have spoken unto you.
John 15:3*

After offering a sacrifice, the priest would go to the Brass Laver — a big wash basin — to remove the splattering of blood and any dirt he had on him. So too, working my way through the Tabernacle, this is where I wash in the water as well.

What water?

Jesus said, "Now you are clean through the Word which I have spoken unto you" (John 15:3).

"How shall a young man cleanse his way?" David asked. "By taking heed to the Word" (Psalm 119:9).

Paul taught that we, as the church, are cleansed "with the washing of water by the word" (Ephesians 5:26).

The Brass Laver is where I stop and "wash myself" in the Word by reflecting on one or two verses. You see, the inside of the Laver was made of the mirrors the Israelites brought with them out of Egypt (Exodus 12:36, 38:8). Therefore, when the priest looked in the Laver, he could see his reflection and wash accordingly.

So too, James likens the Word to a mirror (James 1:23). As I open the Word, I allow the Lord to minister a few verses to me. And as I begin to fellowship with Him, I feel refreshed and cleansed by Him just as surely as the priests experienced refreshment and cleansing at the Laver.

This is not the time I study or read through the Word. Rather, I simply think about and meditate on a verse or two that is on my mind or that I know from memory. For example, in John 14, Jesus says, "Let not your heart be troubled. Believe in Me." So, as I converse with Him at the Laver, I say, "Thank You, Lord, that I don't have to allow my heart to be troubled. You've given me a choice — and I choose right now to not allow my heart to be troubled today."

Growing up, I learned that having devotions — a time of Bible reading and prayer — was vital. So, for many years, I did just that. I would read my Bible and then I would pray. While that's not wrong, it would be similar to calling my wife and saying, "Tammy, I'm going to talk, talk, talk. Then you talk, talk, talk and we'll be done."

That's the way I used to have devotions. "Lord," I'd say, "You talk to me in the Word. Then I'll talk to You through prayer."

How much better it would be to interact — for me to talk and for Tammy to respond; for Tammy to talk and for me to respond. So too, how much better for me to listen to my Father as He speaks to me through a portion of a verse and then respond in prayer to that which He says to me before going on to the next verse.

As you talk to the Lord, I strongly suggest that you pray out loud. I find that when I don't pray audibly, my mind tends to wander and I begin thinking about everything from the leaky faucet I hear dripping to the sound of the planes flying overhead. If you put your thoughts in sentence form and pray out loud, however, your heart will be focused and your mind will be kept from wandering.

I have also found that I don't need to talk rapid-fire with the Lord. Instead, I can have a very relaxed relationship with Him. I can offer a sentence of prayer and then rest for a moment or two. We mistakenly think that we have to keep our sentences flowing because, if we're in public, people will think we're either stuttering or that we don't know how to pray. All too often, we needlessly carry that pressure into our private prayer lives.

I encourage you to take your time. Slow down — and enjoy a relaxed conversation with the Lord as you talk over that verse or two you are reflecting on here at the Brass Laver.

Step 5
The Table of Showbread

∾   ∾   ∾   ∾   ∾

The place of petition

Give us this day our daily bread.
Matthew 6:11

Now we enter the Tabernacle (the tent) itself. As we do, we see on the right the Table of Showbread containing twelve loaves of bread the priests would eat to satisfy their own hunger.

Peter tells us that we are also all members

of a holy priesthood (1 Peter 2:5). So at the Table of Showbread, I pray for my own needs.

"Isn't that selfish?" you ask.

Not at all. You see, the old adage is true: Blessings are like measles; you can't give 'em unless you got 'em! If I'm going to be a blessing to my kids at home, to the people in my neighborhood, to my friends at work, I need to be blessed myself. Therefore, I freely and frankly say, "Father, I have needs."

When the Pharisees accused Jesus' disciples of breaking the Law when they plucked grain on the Sabbath (Matthew 12), Jesus referred them to the account in 1 Samuel 21, where David was given bread from the Table of Showbread to sustain him as he fled from Saul. In other words, Jesus condemned neither David nor His disciples for having needs or being cognizant of [*aware of*] their needs.

The problem is not with having needs.

The problem lies in to whom or where we go to meet them. Our Heavenly Father knows we have need of "all these things" (Matthew 6:32), and He alone is the One who can supply them (Philippians 4:19).

In regard to praying for my needs, I have discovered the benefits of keeping a journal to record my requests.

For example, imagine you're at the Table of Showbread, praying for a raise. A week later, when raises are announced and your name isn't on the list, your heart sinks. But that's because you forgot about the time two months earlier when you prayed, "Lord, free me from the pull of the materialistic tendency that arises so easily within me. Keep me in a place of total dependence upon You so that I might walk by faith."

"Lord, help me to be more patient," we pray passionately.

"Okay," the Lord says. "I'll be happy to

answer that prayer."

"Lord, the person who sits next to me at work is driving me crazy," we pray a week later. "Can't You help him find a different job?"

"No," the Lord says. "He's the very answer to the prayer you prayed last week to be more patient."

When I keep a journal, I see how my prayers can contradict each other. Keeping a record of my prayers allows me to say, "Lord, thank You that You're doing what I asked for then, which explains why this other thing is or isn't happening now."

I encourage you to experiment with keeping a prayer journal. You might find that it answers a whole lot of questions for you.

"My God shall supply all your needs," Paul declares (Philippians 4:19). The Table of Showbread speaks of the desire and ability of our Father to do just that.

After all, He has already given us His best, the "Bread of Life" - His Son, so anything else we ask for is a piece of cake in comparison!

The Golden Candlestick

ॐ　ॐ　ॐ　ॐ　ॐ

The place of ministry

Let your light so shine before men,
that they may see your good works,
and glorify your Father
which is in heaven.
Matthew 5:16

The second piece of furniture within the Tabernacle itself was the Golden Candlestick. As seen in Revelation 2 and 3, the Candlestick speaks of churches and ministries. Therefore, this is where I pray for ministry: ministries I'm directly part of, ministries I'm familiar with, ministries I read about in the paper, or even ministries different from my flavor, background, or preference. I pray for churches and pastors by name. I pray for foreign missions and for other organizations that preach Jesus.

Why?

When David was fighting against the Amalekites after the Ziklag attack, two hundred of his men couldn't go to the front lines. Instead, they stayed behind and guarded the supplies. When David and his men returned victorious, those who went with David into battle said, "We'll split the spoils only between us."

"Not so," David said. "The guys on the supply lines will be rewarded to the same degree that you are" (1 Samuel 30).

This means that when you pray for other ministries, by keeping the "supply lines" open, you participate in that ministry and will share in its reward when you stand before the Lord.

I pray for ministers and ministries — locally, regionally, and internationally — not only because without prayer their effectiveness will be diminished, but also because I'll get to share in the rewards and blessings of what the Lord does through them!

Isaiah tells us that the nation of Israel was to be a light to the Gentiles (Isaiah 60:1-2). In other words, the reason Israel was initially created was to show the whole world how to know God and how to walk with Him. So too, as believers, it is our privilege and responsibility to pray for ministries that shed light on what it means to know God and to walk with Him.

If you're looking for rewards, if you want to hear God say, "Well done," I encourage you to spend time at the Golden Candlestick. Pray for the lights of the world — not just the one you're involved in, not just those of your flavor, but for all kinds of ministries. Not only will your prayers affect the ministries you're praying for, but your prayers will also have a powerful altering effect on your own perspective about churches and denominations different than yours. And you will find yourself being enlightened and ignited in a new way in your love for all of His family, the entire Church in totality.

Step 7
The Altar of Incense

෴ ෴ ෴ ෴ ෴

The place of intercession

*... pray for them which
despitefully use you ...*
Matthew 5:44

The third object inside the Tabernacle was the Altar of Incense. According to Revelation 8, the Altar of Incense speaks of intercession.

This is where I intercede, or pray, for people. I keep a list and go right down it, praying for people by name. I pray for my family, my friends, my neighbors, my brothers and sisters in Christ — and for my enemies (Matthew 5:44).

My "enemies" list is really, really small. Why?

Because I've learned a secret. That is, when I pray for enemies — people who irritate me or who I feel have wronged me in some way — my heart changes toward them and they don't remain my enemies for very long. You see, an interesting thing happens when I pray for people who bug me. First, God answers prayer and they may very well begin to change. But more importantly, God changes me. I find my heart softening toward them. I receive insights about them. I become involved with them via intercession.

Now when you pray for your "enemies," please remember the words of Jesus who said, "Do unto others as you would have them do unto you" (Matthew 7:12). How do you want people to pray for you? Do you want them to pray, "Lord, humble him today. Break him that he might see how wrong he is"? When people pray for me, I want them to say, "Lord, be merciful to Jon. Be gracious. Be kind. He's a little slow, You know." If that's how I want to be prayed for, I must pray for others in the same way.

"But I can't pray for her that way," you might protest. "She has hurt me too badly."

I understand. But consider this: Although you can't change how you feel about her, you can change how you think about her. God can change your heart, but He won't change your mind. However, if you change your mind, God will change your heart. How do you change your mind?

You say, "Lord, You taught me to pray for, to forgive, and to love my enemies. Therefore, I choose to do that right now. Bless him. Encourage her. Amaze them with Your grace today."

And, sure enough, as I spend time at the Altar of Incense, as I change my mind and pray for my enemies, God is faithful to change my own heart every time.

Step 8

The Holy of Holies

$\approx$ $\approx$ $\approx$ $\approx$ $\approx$

The place of worship

*And thou shalt put the mercy seat upon the
ark of the testimony in the most holy place.
Exodus 26:34*

The last stop in the Tabernacle is beyond the
veil into the Holy of Holies wherein dwelt
the *chabod* — the visible, tangible presence of
God. Inside the Holy of Holies was the ark of the
covenant — a two foot by three foot box covered

by the mercy seat, over which the Shekinah glory of God, the *chabod*, rested.

Only the high priest, only on the Day of Atonement, could enter the Holy of Holies. And if he did so with any unconfessed sin, he died. But when Jesus cried, "It is finished!" the veil separating the Holy of Holies was ripped from top to bottom. It was as if God declared, "Open House! Any man, every man, can come into My presence at any time because the blood of My Son has cleansed you perfectly and completely."

Therefore, because of the finished work of the cross, even I, sinful man that I am, can experience the glory, the *chabod*, the presence of God. This is where I worship. How do I worship? I wait on the Lord. What does it mean to wait on the Lord?

Suppose you went to a restaurant and the waiter told you what you should order. Wouldn't you say, or at least think, "Wait a minute. I'm the customer. You're the waiter. I'll order what I want. I'm not here to serve you. You're here to serve me"? So too, to wait on the Lord means to let Him order what He wants from the menu of worship found in the Book of Psalms ...

"Come let us worship and bow down."

"Clap your hands, all ye people."

"Shout unto God with a voice of triumph."

"Be still and know that I am God."

"Sing praise unto the Lord and bless His name."

Singing, shouting, and silence; bowing before Him and standing in awe of Him are among the expressions God has ordered. Worship isn't about what I like. I'm the waiter. Worship is about what God desires. Therefore, in the Holy of Holies, I open Psalms, the workbook on worship, and say, "Lord, I lift my hands as Your Word tells me to do. I bow my knees in adoration of You."

I lift my hands, sometimes bow my knees, sometimes lie prostrate on the floor. Sometimes I'll just sit quietly. Other times, I'll pray in the Spirit or sing loudly. In all of these ways and more, I find myself reveling in the *chabod*, the reality, the presence of God.

Personal Application

$\approx$ $\approx$ $\approx$ $\approx$ $\approx$

At this point in our journey, I must remind you of something that is essential. You see, because of the finished work of the cross, we don't *need* to go through the Gates of thanksgiving or the Courts of praise to experience the presence of God. We are not *required* to stop at the Brass Altar or the Brass Laver. Nor are we *obligated* to spend time at the Table of Showbread or the Altar of Incense. For the veil is rent, ripped open from top to bottom. We can enter freely into the Holy of Holies immediately, confidently, at any time, you see.

But, personally, I have found each of these "stops" helpful in softening my heart and sharpening my focus to be able to enter His presence.

You see, the Father is not reluctant to allow us access to Him. The problem is with our inability to perceive His presence. And I have found that the paradigm of praying through the Tabernacle solves this problem in a very practical and potent way.

Depending on the schedule or the needs of any given day, the amount of time I spend at each "stop" varies. I have prayed through the Tabernacle between appointments on busy days. Other times, I have had the luxury of spending longer periods of unhurried time as I make my way from the Gate of the Courtyard to the Holy of Holies in the Tabernacle. Sometimes, the needs of others are so pressing that I linger longer at the Altar of Incense. Other times, I am so overwhelmed with gratitude that I barely get past the Gate.

Regardless of the time spent, praying through the Tabernacle enables me to say, "I have thanked God for what He's done for me; I have acknowledged His greatness; I have confessed my sin; I have meditated on His Word; I have spread my needs before Him; I have prayed for ministries and family; I have spent time enjoying His presence."

And, rather than leaving my prayer time feeling guilty about my wandering thoughts or sleepy spirit, I feel as though the Lord has allowed me to truly accomplish some things in prayer — and often to accomplish other things as well ...

I used to hate to mow the lawn — until I realized I could redeem the time by praying through the Tabernacle as I mowed. On the first strip, I enter His Gates with thanksgiving and thank the Lord for everything I can think of.

On the second strip, I enter His Courts with praise, thanking Him for who He is.

On the third strip, I confess my sins (Brass Altar).

On the fourth strip, I meditate on a verse or two (Brass Laver).

On the fifth strip, I pray for my specific

needs (Table of Showbread).

On the sixth strip, I pray for ministries (Golden Candlestick).

On the seventh strip, I pray for my family, friends — and enemies (Altar of Incense).

On the eighth strip, I worship the Lord — singing and rejoicing in His presence (Holy of Holies).

As I do this, what was once a job is transformed into joy!

When I was single after my first wife went home to be with the Lord, I used to clean house late at night after I got home from church. I used to hate it — until I discovered early on in my three year stint that I could enter (Step 1) His Gates with thanksgiving as I vacuumed the hallway. Then, I could enter (Step 2) into His Courts with praise as I cleaned the living room. In the bathroom (Step 3 - Brass Laver), I confessed my sin — a good place for that! Then on to the kitchen, where I washed dishes and meditated (Step 4) at the Brass Laver. In the dining room, I prayed (Step 5 - Table of Showbread) for my needs. Straightening the family room, I prayed (Step 6 - Golden Candlestick) for God's family and church ministries. Then, into the bedrooms, I prayed (Step 7 - Altar of Incense) for my children, family, friends, etc. And then, even though the hour was late, I was refreshed and renewed as I entered into the Holy of Holies (Step 8) worshipping the Lord and calling it a day. Incredibly, I actually began to look forward to house cleaning every night, for you see, it was no longer just a chore; it was a unique opportunity to spend time with my Lord.

I used to dread running laps on the elementary school track behind my house — until I discovered that I could enter the Gates of the Tabernacle with thanksgiving on the first lap, audibly thanking the Lord for His goodness to me.

Lap 2: I envision the Courtyard and praise God for who He is.

Lap 3: I imagine the Brass Altar and confess my sins specifically. (I slow down on this lap!)

Lap 4: I imagine the Brass Laver and then meditate on a portion of the Word.

Lap 5: I picture the Table of Showbread and pray for my needs.

Lap 6: I see in my mind's eye the Golden Candlestick and pray for ministers and missionaries, for evangelists and elders — for all those who shine the light of the gospel into a dark world.

Lap 7: I see the Altar of Incense and pray for my family, my neighbors, my friends — and my enemies.

Lap 8: I'm in a perfect place to enter the Holy of Holies and worship the Lord. (Indeed, it's my last lap!)

When I'm done, I not only have two miles under my belt but the presence of God in my heart.

Dear brother, precious sister, I encourage you to pray through the Tabernacle as you clean the house or mow the lawn, run laps or commute to work — and see if prayer doesn't become a joy once again.

"Pray without ceasing," Paul wrote to the Thessalonians. And his decree became my delight when I realized I could pray with clarity even as I tended to the needs of any given day.

Do I always pray through the Tabernacle?

No.

But it is a tool I use regularly when I hit those stale, difficult sessions of prayer that come my way not infrequently. If you spend three or four minutes at each one of these stops, not only will it be the fastest thirty minutes you've spent in prayer — but you won't leave your prayer time wondering what you prayed about.

Whether or not you use this pattern, however, my greatest prayer is that the desire of our hearts increasingly might be that of the disciples when they said,

"Lord, teach us to pray."

Summary

❧ ❧ ❧ ❧ ❧

Praying through the Tabernacle

The Gate
Thank God for what He does

The Courtyard
Praise God for who He is

The Brass Altar
*Confess specific sins and
confess that you are forgiven*

The Brass Laver
*Let the Lord speak to you
through a verse or two of Scripture*

The Table of Showbread
Talk to the Lord about personal needs

The Golden Candlestick
*Pray for ministers and missionaries — for all
who shine God's light*

The Altar of Incense
Pray for your family, friends, and enemies

The Holy of Holies
*Worship the Lord with a heart in tune with
His presence*